793.73   Munro, Roxie.
MUN
          Mazeways.

$12.95   000046662
                         12/31/2007
                    DATE

MAZEWAYS

A TO Z

by Roxie Munro

STERLING
New York / London

To SOPHIE GRACE WOOD

STERLING and the distinctive Sterling logo
are registered trademarks of Sterling Publishing Co., Inc.

Library of Congress Cataloging-in-Publication Data
Munro, Roxie.
  Mazeways : A to Z / Roxie Munro.
    p. cm.
  ISBN-13: 978-1-4027-3774-9
  ISBN-10: 1-4027-3774-2
  1. Maze puzzles. I. Title.

GV1507.M3M87 2007
793.73'8—dc22

                          2007001586

10 9 8 7 6 5 4 3 2 1

Published by Sterling Publishing Co., Inc.
387 Park Avenue South, New York, NY 10016
© 2007 by Roxie Munro
Designed by Lauren Rille
The artwork for this book was prepared using black and colored inks on Strathmore paper.
Distributed in Canada by Sterling Publishing
℅ Canadian Manda Group, 165 Dufferin Street, Toronto, Ontario, Canada M6K 3H6
Distributed in the United Kingdom by GMC Distribution Services, Castle Place,
166 High Street, Lewes, East Sussex, England BN7 1XU
Distributed in Australia by Capricorn Link (Australia) Pty. Ltd., P.O. Box 704, Windsor, NSW 2756, Australia

Sterling ISBN-13: 978-1-4027-3774-9
       ISBN-10: 1-4027-3774-2

For information about custom editions, special sales, premium and corporate purchases,
please contact Sterling Special Sales Department at 800-805-5489 or specialsales@sterlingpub.com.

Welcome to Mazeways!

A is for Airport, **B** is for Boatyard, **C** is for Circus...and on to **Z**oo!

Every letter forms its own maze, and each of these alpha-adventures comes with directions that guide you through from start to finish. Use your finger to find your way. Just make sure you stay on the paths or roads, and always use the shortest route. Navigate these mazes as you would in real life: drive your car on the right side of the road, cross the street only at a crosswalk, and feel free to walk around landmarks or furniture, as long as there's nothing to block your way.

There are also more than 700 interesting things to find in these pages—crocodiles and rattlesnakes, dump trucks and motorcycles, baseball diamonds, sunken treasure, and more! Find them all, and then use this book to make up games of your own to play.

Have fun exploring these mazeways!

Roxie Munro

Look for the puzzle answers at the back.

We're cleared to land!

Bring your airliner down for a landing at the **AIRPORT** and then taxi it to Gate A4. Next, guide the orange private plane from its hangar to the oil tanker truck to refuel. Take off on Runway 09.

Find a radio antenna, a wind sock, 10 airplanes, a helicopter, a radar tower, an American flag, a yellow taxi, an oil tanker truck, 2 parking lots, 5 airplane hangars, a weathervane, and an air traffic control tower.

You won the race!

Congratulations! Now sail your red boat from the finish line to the **BOATYARD** dock, tie up between two blue boats, and then walk over to the clubhouse to receive your trophy.

Find a channel buoy, 4 boat trailers, 2 sculls, a water skier, 3 people fishing, a volleyball game, an American flag, a boat ramp, 2 beach umbrellas, an anchor, 2 gas pumps, 8 racing sailboats, a lighthouse, 4 canoes, 7 picnic tables, and a ship's wheel.

Make way for the elephants!

Ride on the lead elephant to the center of the
CIRCUS ring. Take a picture of the Human Pyramid,
and borrow a unicycle. Ride out of the ring and grab
a red balloon as you exit the Big Top.

Find 5 balloons, 2 tigers, 3 poodles, 13 clowns,
14 hats, a bicycle rider, 2 horses, 3 unicycles,
a hula-hoop lady, a clown car, and a seal.

Busy day in the West

From the **DESERT** mesa, ride your horse down the rutted dirt road. Stop at the chuck wagon for a quick bite, fill your canteen at the water barrel, then search the paths to find the lost calf. He could really use a drink!

Find 2 cowboys, 6 grazing cattle, a red-tailed hawk, a mesa, a crossroads sign, a coyote, a roadrunner, a fence gate, a lost calf, a rattlesnake, a chuck wagon cook, a water barrel, and a jackrabbit.

It's a masterpiece!

Pay the **EXHIBITION** entrance fee and go into the gallery. Admire the painting with the colorful stripes, and then find a sailboat picture. End up in front of your favorite painting—the bowl of apples.

Find 3 guards, 5 sculptures, 3 glass cases, 5 benches, and a queen, a horse and a lighthouse.

Fire on Main Street!

Slide down the FIREHOUSE pole, grab a quick drink of water, and put on your boots, jacket, and helmet. Call for backup on the telephone. Check the town map on the computer, and jump on the back of the ladder truck.

Find a Dalmatian, a clock, a water cooler, 5 traffic cones, a fire extinguisher, a computer, fire station trophies, 4 pairs of gloves, 4 helmets, 4 jackets, a phone, a coffee mug, a pair of glasses, and a siren.

Perfect day for a picnic!

Enter the **GARDEN** through the main gate near the big white house and make your way along the paths to the pier. Hop in a canoe and paddle across the pond to the picnic table area.

Find 13 park benches, 2 fountains, 3 deer, public restrooms, a statue, a tractor, a carousel, 3 canoes, 4 weeping willow trees, and a gazebo.

School's out!

You're a driver. Pick up the children at school in your bus and take them home via the Route 4 exit on the HIGHWAY. Then hop in your milk truck and drive it back to the school to deliver fresh milk for lunch tomorrow.

Find 4 school buses, a milk truck, 3 horses, a bicycle, a person fishing, a baseball diamond, 3 motorcycles, 11 cows, a swing set, a tractor, 4 city buses, a dump truck, an oil tanker truck, 2 seesaws, 3 fence gates, 2 sets of bleachers, a slide, and an American flag.

Let's go camping!

From the blue van, walk to the pier and row a boat to the **ISLAND** dock. Check out the view from the lighthouse, take a break at the public restrooms, then make your way to the campground.

Find a water skier, a lighthouse, 3 green park benches, 5 sailboats, 2 bridges, 10 picnic tables, 2 umbrellas, 4 canoes, 4 people fishing, and a restaurant.

It's a jungle out there!

Leave your red van at the sandy beach. Travel by foot and canoe to the fishing pier via the river and the **JUNGLE** paths.

Find 3 canoes, 4 bridges, 2 flamingos, 3 piers, 4 picnic tables, a coiled snake, a waterfall, a crocodile, and 2 people fishing.

Your customer's waiting!

Quick! Enter the **KITCHEN** through the dining room door. Grab a hamburger, a bag of potato chips, a piece of cake, lettuce and tomato side order, and a soda from the refrigerator. Go back out to deliver the order.

Find 6 loaves of bread, a tray of cookies, a pie, a microwave oven, 2 cakes, 3 trash cans, a toaster, 2 coffee machines, and a roll of paper towels.

Rome, here I come!

Enter through the **LIBRARY** door. Find the red Italian language book hidden on a shelf. Look up flights to Rome on the computer. Find Italy on the globe, and then check out your book from the librarian.

Find a book cart, 4 computers, a trash can, a globe, 4 pairs of glasses, a backpack, a magazine rack, and 2 black pens.

Gear up for a hike!

From the road on the left, climb the **MOUNTAIN** peaks, using bridges and rowboats if necessary, and then wind your way down the other side of the far peak.

Find 3 tunnels, 3 deer, a person fishing, a Big Horn sheep, a ladder, an umbrella, 3 piers, 3 waterfalls, 4 boats, and 5 picnic tables.

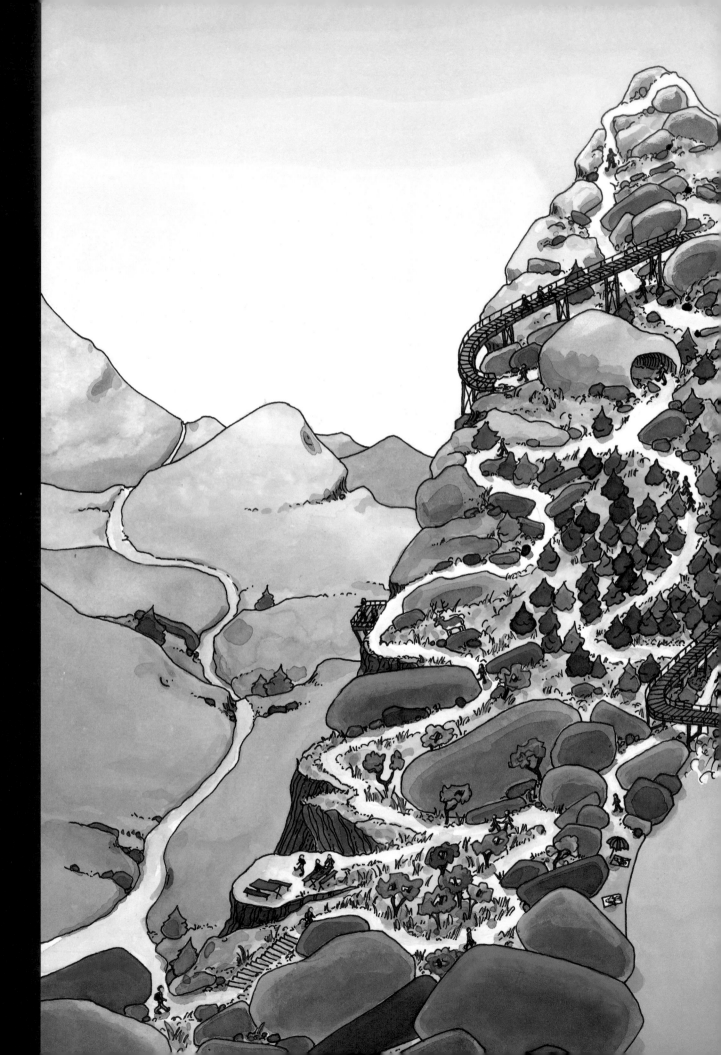

Your turn to pick the holiday tree!

Go in the front entrance of the plant NURSERY through the gift shop. Choose a wreath with a red bow, then find the decorated tree. Take the tree and wreath to your orange pickup truck in the parking lot.

Find 2 red sawhorses, 2 baby carriages, 2 shovels, 2 pickup trucks, 2 wheelbarrows, a fish, a bicycle, and 2 benches.

It's apple-picking time!

Carry the basket of apples through the **ORCHARD** to the farmhouse. Then get back on the path to the picnic table for lunch.

Find 3 cows, a pier, a barn, a bridge, a park bench, a horse, a tractor, a ladder, 4 gates, a dog, a picnic table, and a pickup truck.

New shoes for school!

Drive into the mall **PARKING LOT** and park in the space between two red cars. Walk to the restaurant for lunch. After eating, go shoe shopping, then get a cart and pick up some snacks at the grocery store.

Find an apple, a black top hat, a hamburger, 2 gold stars, 18 streetlights, a carrot, 2 big shoes, and a motorcycle.

Don't forget your hardhat!

Enter the **QUARRY** from the highway and park by the green pickup truck. Then find the small blue wheelbarrow, fill it with red bags of gravel, and take them to the boss's gray trailer.

Find 2 cranes, 2 dump trucks, a steam shovel, 3 ladders, 2 entrance ramps, and a gray trailer.

A long, hard day, and more to do...

Ride in on the mountain trail, go through the main RANCH gate, and check on the mare and the foal in the corral. Unsaddle your horse at the barn. Next, fix the tractor. Then pick some apples and take them to the picnic tables for a snack.

Find 14 horses, a mesa, 3 pigs, a windmill, an American flag, a riding ring, 13 cows, a ladder, a deer, an armadillo, a chuck wagon, a bull, a clothesline, a tractor, 3 picnic tables, 4 chickens, a coyote, a horse trailer, and a scarecrow.

Race you downhill!

Take the longest lift to the mountain top and ski downhill all the way. Continue cross-country to the **SKI RESORT** lodge for a cup of hot chocolate.

Find a lake, a hawk, 2 deer, a snowman, 3 swans, a summit snack shack, a bear, 5 picnic tables, a class of beginners, and 5 snowboarders.

The bus is late again!

From the bright green bus stop near the yellow house, ride the school bus into **TOWN**, all the way to school.

Find 2 baseball diamonds, 2 American flags, a fountain, 9 cows, 6 picnic tables, 3 school buses, a movie theater, a dump truck, 5 home swimming pools, the town's big pool, a playground, a tractor, and a motorcycle.

Treasure awaits in the deep!

You're all decked out in your scuba gear. Without running into any fish or plant life **UNDERWATER**, check out the octopus, and find the sunken treasure chest. Bring some gold coins up to the research boat.

Find 4 dolphins, 2 brain corals, an octopus, 3 stingrays, a starfish, a trumpet fish, a sea horse, a shark's tail, a spotted moray eel, a sunken treasure chest, and an old anchor.

Grab your backpack!

From the signpost, hike your way up, down, and across the deep **VALLEY** to meet your friends at the picnic area.

Find 7 bridges, 2 park benches, a green trash can, a helicopter, a tunnel, 4 picnic tables, a coyote, 2 public restrooms, 3 deer, a hot-air balloon, and a jet plane.

Can't wait to ride those rapids!

Starting at the overnight camp, cross over the **WATERFALLS** to the Wild River Ride, and zoom down the rapids on your raft.

Find 2 benches, a rocky river crossing, 3 green trash cans, 5 picnic tables, 3 deer, 3 birds, 2 tents, 3 bridges, and 4 rafts.

Happy birthday to you!

From your yellow house, drive to the riding ring and take a lesson on your favorite horse. Cross the tracks at the railroad **X-ING** near the school. Pick up your cousin at the train station, then go home to your backyard birthday party.

Find a tractor, a train, 3 American flags, 2 barns, 2 baseball diamonds, 4 horses, 4 cows, 3 school buses, 4 swimming pools, 5 balloons, and a clock.

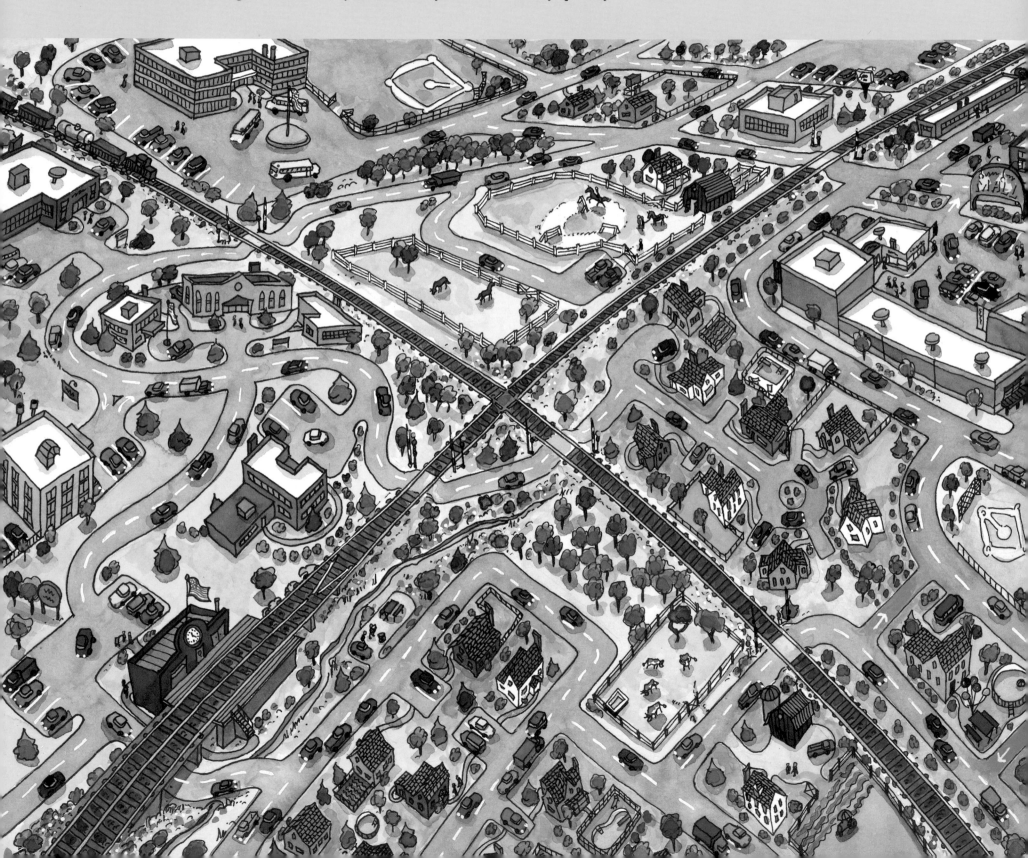

I'll meet you in the tree house!

Enter the **YARD** from the driveway. Get the hose from the shed and water the garden. Scoop out the pool toys. Get dog food from the bag on the patio table and feed the dog. Meet your best friend in the tree house.

Find a duck, 2 bicycles, a seesaw, a sandbox, 3 buckets, a barbecue grill, a cat, a fish, a rake, an umbrella, a bird feeder, 6 socks, a picnic table, a squirrel, a beach ball, and gardening gloves.

Zookeeper for the day!

From the main entrance, bike to the **ZOO** parking lot and lock up your bike. Check on the hippos, then feed the kangaroos and the gorillas. Take a break for an ice cream cone. Study the elephants and the zebras, then finally check out the reptile house.

Find the giraffes, flamingos, 2 fountains, penguins, a cheetah, tigers, the monkey house, lions, 12 umbrellas, alligators, polar bears, ostriches, yaks, camels, 2 picnic tables, rhinos, 18 park benches, and a balloon.

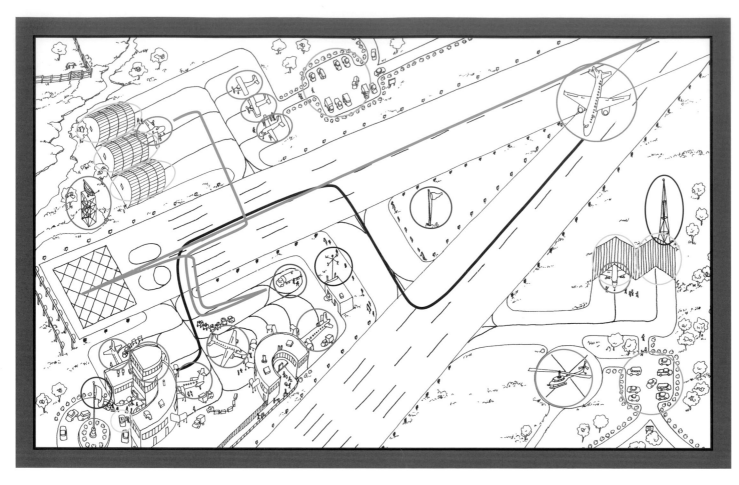

A

a radio antenna
a wind sock
10 airplanes
a helicopter
a radar tower
an American flag
a yellow taxi
an oil tanker truck
2 parking lots
5 airplane hangars
a weathervane
an air traffic control tower

B

a channel buoy
4 boat trailers
2 sculls
a water skier
3 people fishing
a volleyball game
an American flag
a boat ramp
2 beach umbrellas
an anchor
2 gas pumps
8 racing sailboats
a lighthouse
4 canoes
7 picnic tables
a ship's wheel

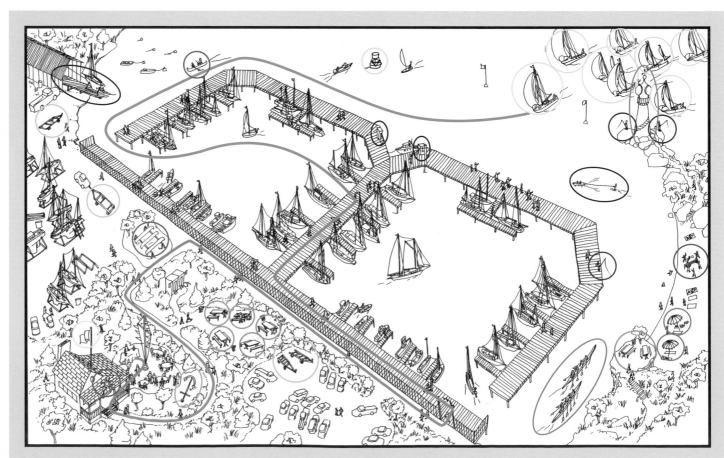

C

5 balloons, 2 tigers, 3 poodles, 13 clowns, 14 hats, a bicycle rider, 2 horses, 3 unicycles, a hula-hoop lady, a clown car, a seal

D

2 cowboys, 6 grazing cattle, a red-tailed hawk, a mesa, a crossroads sign, a coyote, a roadrunner, a fence gate, a lost calf, a rattlesnake, a chuck wagon cook, a water barrel, a jackrabbit

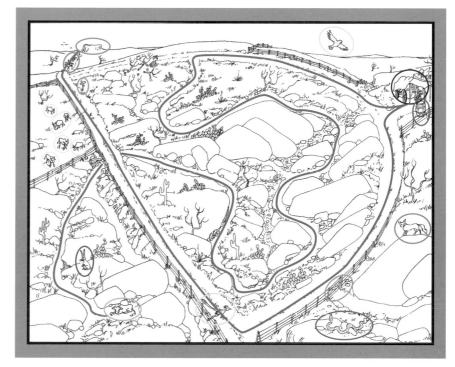

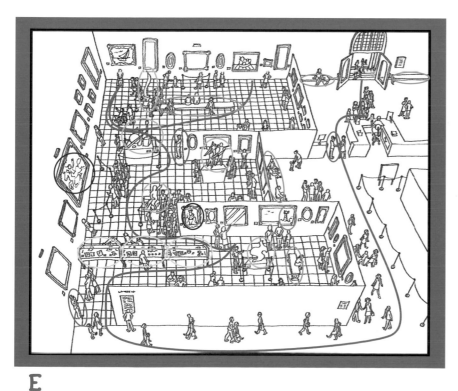

E

3 guards, 5 sculptures, 3 glass cases, 5 benches, a queen, a horse, a lighthouse

F

a Dalmatian, a clock, a water cooler, 5 traffic cones, a fire extinguisher, a computer, fire station trophies, 4 pairs of gloves, 4 helmets, 4 jackets, a phone, a coffee mug, a pair of glasses, a siren

G

13 park benches
2 fountains
3 deer
public restrooms
a statue
a tractor
a carousel
3 canoes
4 weeping willow trees
a gazebo

H

4 school buses
a milk truck
3 horses
a bicycle
a person fishing
a baseball diamond
3 motorcycles
11 cows
a swing set
a tractor
4 city buses
a dump truck
an oil tanker truck
2 seesaws
3 fence gates
2 sets of bleachers
a slide
an American flag

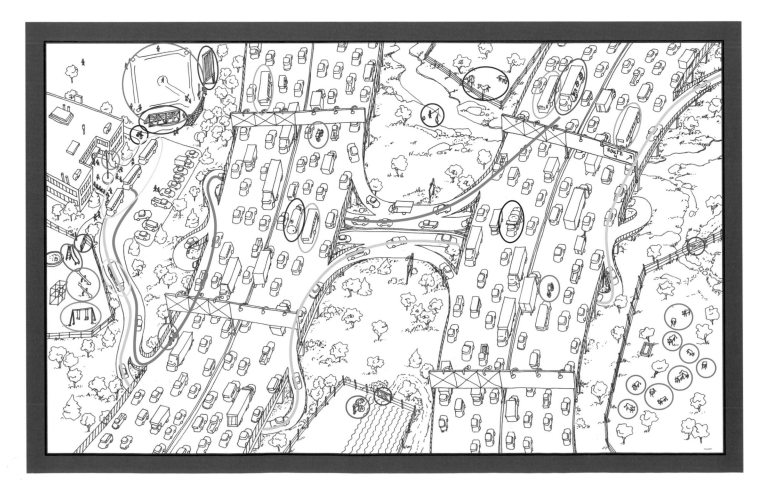

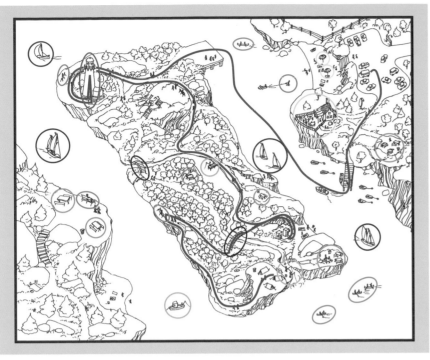

I

a water skier, a lighthouse, 3 green park benches, 5 sailboats, 2 bridges, 10 picnic tables, 2 umbrellas, 4 canoes, 4 people fishing, a restaurant

J

3 canoes, 4 bridges, 2 flamingos, 3 piers, 4 picnic tables, a coiled snake, a waterfall, a crocodile, 2 people fishing

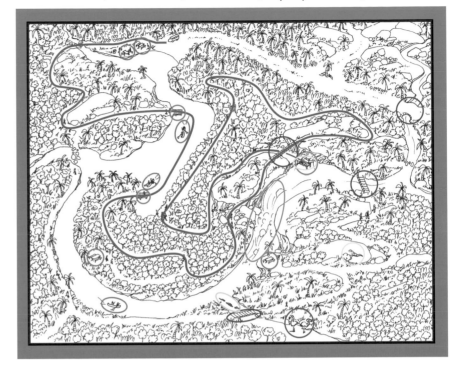

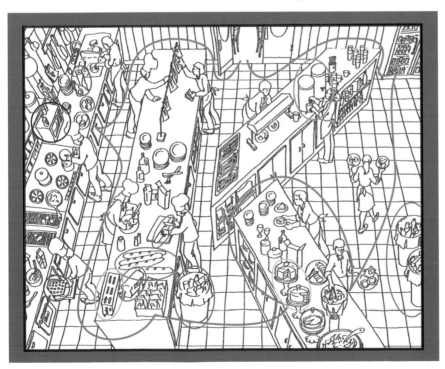

K

6 loaves of bread, a tray of cookies, a pie, a microwave oven, 2 cakes, 3 trash cans, a toaster, 2 coffee machines, a roll of paper towels

L

a book cart, 4 computers, a trash can, a globe, 4 pairs of glasses, a backpack, a magazine rack, 2 black pens

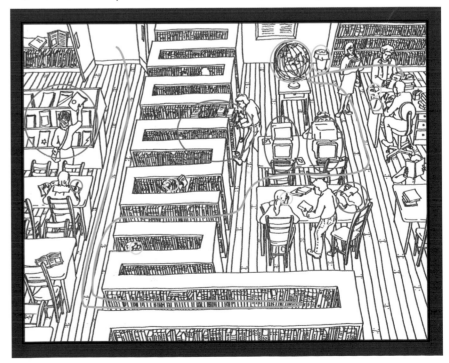

M

3 tunnels
3 deer
a person fishing
a Big Horn sheep
a ladder
an umbrella
3 piers
3 waterfalls
4 boats
5 picnic tables

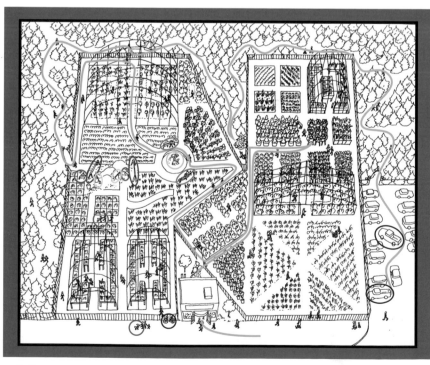

N

2 red sawhorses, 2 baby carriages, 2 shovels, 2 pickup trucks,
2 wheelbarrows, a fish, a bicycle, 2 benches

O

3 cows, a pier, a barn, a bridge, a park bench, a horse,
a tractor, a ladder, 4 gates, a dog, a picnic table,
a pickup truck

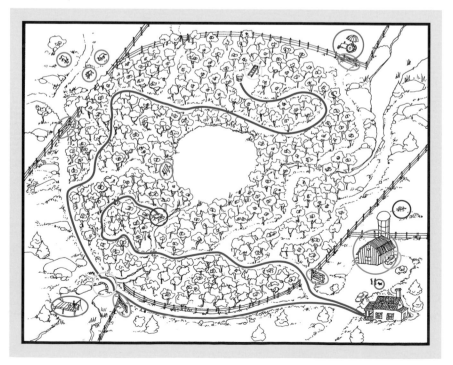

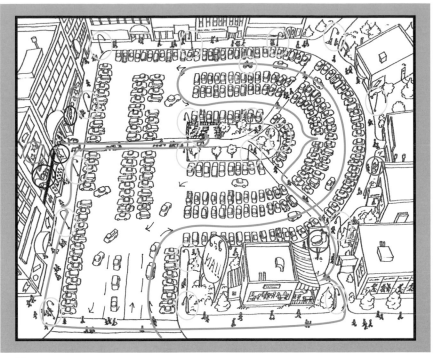

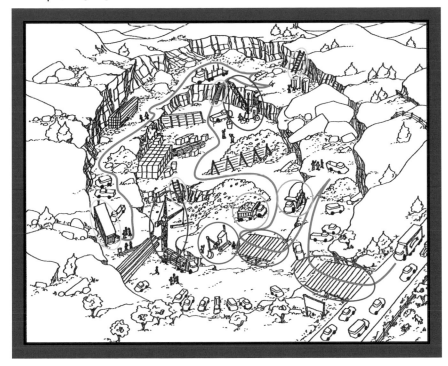

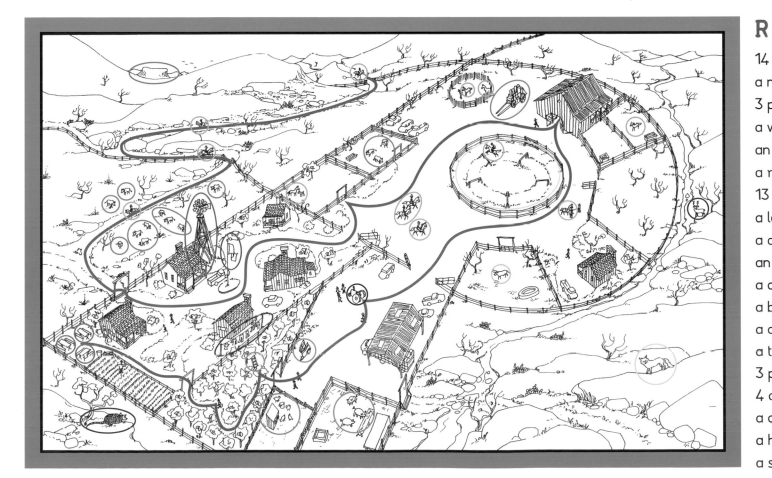

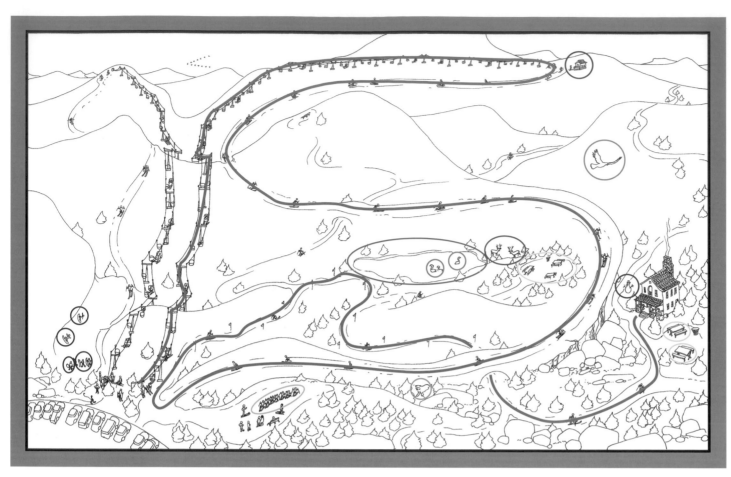

S

a lake

a hawk

2 deer

a snowman

3 swans

a summit snack shack

a bear

5 picnic tables

a class of beginners

5 snowboarders

T

2 baseball diamonds

2 American flags

a fountain

9 cows

6 picnic tables

3 school buses

a movie theater

a dump truck

5 home swimming
   pools

the town's big pool

a playground

a tractor

a motorcycle

U

4 dolphins, 2 brain corals, an octopus, 3 stingrays, a starfish, a trumpet fish, a sea horse, a shark's tail, a spotted moray eel, a sunken treasure chest, an old anchor

V

7 bridges, 2 park benches, a green trash can, a helicopter, a tunnel, 4 picnic tables, a coyote, 2 public restrooms, 3 deer, a hot-air balloon, a jet plane

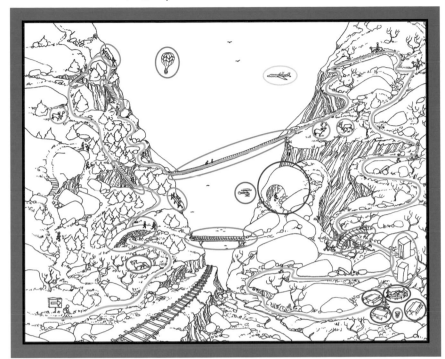

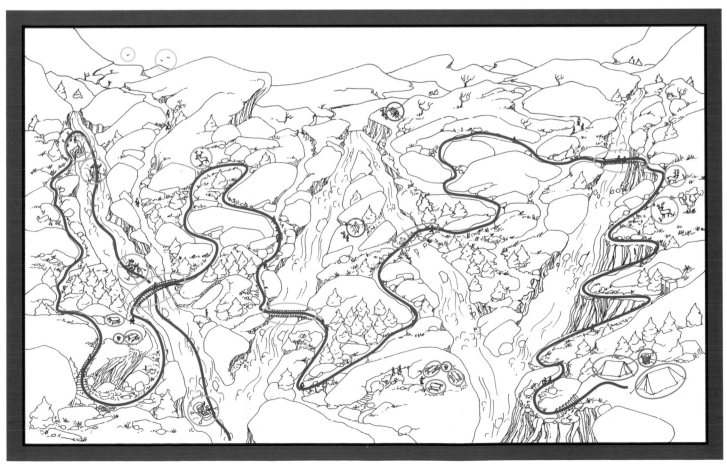

W

2 benches

a rocky river crossing

3 green trash cans

5 picnic tables

3 deer

3 birds

2 tents

3 bridges

4 rafts

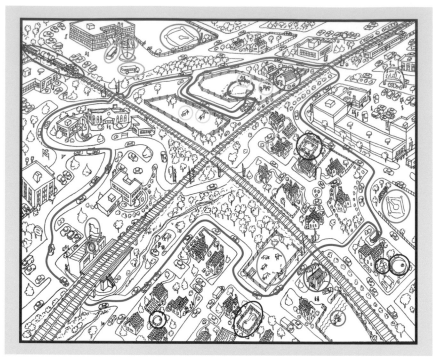

X

a tractor, a train, 3 American flags, 2 barns, 2 baseball diamonds, 4 horses, 4 cows, 3 school buses, 4 swimming pools, 5 balloons, a clock

Y

a duck, 2 bicycles, a seesaw, a sandbox, 3 buckets, a barbecue grill, a cat, a fish, a rake, an umbrella, a bird feeder, 6 socks, a picnic table, a squirrel, a beach ball, gardening gloves

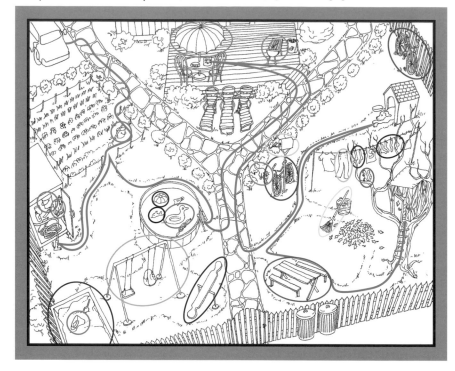

Z

giraffes

flamingos

2 fountains

penguins

a cheetah

tigers

the monkey house

lions

12 umbrellas

alligators

polar bears

ostriches

yaks

camels

2 picnic tables

rhinos

18 park benches

a balloon

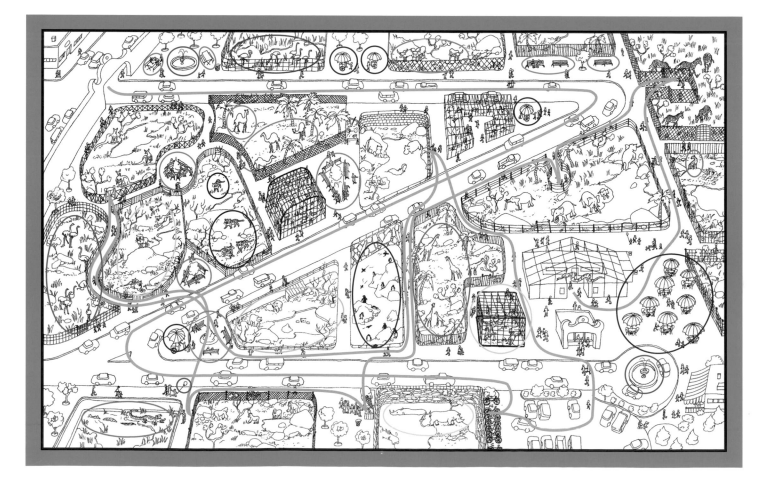